A Black & White
GARDEN

Kay M. Capps Cross

American Quilter's Society

P. O. Box 3290 • Paducah, KY 42002-3290
www.americanquilter.com

The American Quilter's Society (AQS), located in Paducah, Kentucky, is dedicated to promoting the accomplishments of today's quilters. Through its publications and events, AQS strives to honor today's quiltmakers and their work and to inspire future creativity and innovation in quiltmaking.

Text © 2008, Author, Kay M. Capps Cross
Artwork © 2008 American Quilter's Society

Executive Editor: Nicole C. Chambers
Editor: Linda Baxter Lasco
Graphic Design: Lynda Smith
Cover Design: Michael Buckingham
Photography: Charles R. Lynch

American Quilter's Society

P. O. Box 3290 • Paducah, KY 42002-3290 • PHONE: (270) 898-7903 • FAX: (270) 898-1173
www.americanquilter.com

Additional copies of this book may be ordered from the American Quilter's Society, PO Box 3290, Paducah, KY 42002-3290, or online at: www.AmericanQuilter.com.

Library of Congress Cataloging-in-Publication Data

Cross, Kay M. Capps.
  A black & white garden / by Kay M. Capps Cross.
     p. cm.
  Includes bibliographical references and index.
  ISBN 978-1-57432-952-0 (alk. paper)
  1. Patchwork--Patterns. 2. Quilting--Patterns. 3. Black in art. 4. White in art. I. Title.

TT835.C74894 2008
746.46'041--dc22

                    2008003445

Proudly printed and bound in the United States of America.

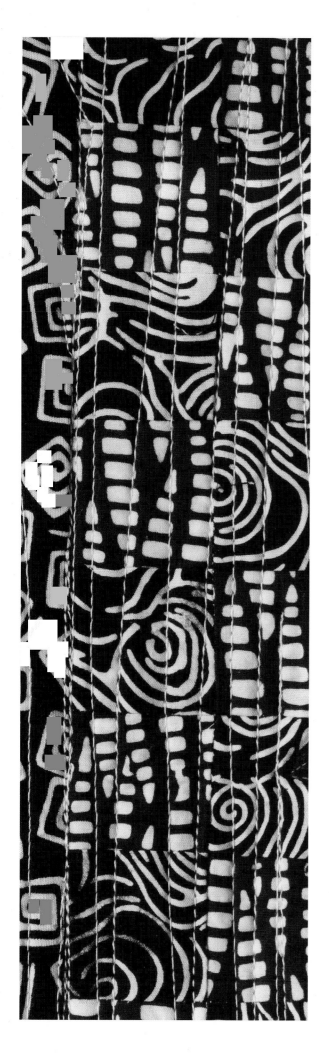

DEDICATION

This book is lovingly dedicated to my children. They enrich my life beyond measure. Not only do they inspire and encourage me, but also by keeping me incredibly busy, they force me to discover easy and fun methods to create the ideas in my head. I thank them for the sleep that incentive affords.

ACKNOWLEDGMENTS

I would like to thank:

- the folks at AQS for continuing on this incredible quilting journey with me.
- the new quilters of the world for continuing this wonderful art form.
- the perpetual quilters of the world for encouraging and inspiring the new quilters.
- the leaders of the quilting industry who paved the way for all of us.
- fabric companies for providing more and more incredible black-and-white fabrics.
- independent quilt shops for carrying those luscious fabrics and supporting our quilting obsessions.
- the Fab Four for allowing me membership in the best club imaginable.
- my family who continues to support and encourage me.
- the binding guru—my beloved Grandma Hap (no, I will not share).
- my children for providing valuable bleacher-bottom development time.
- and my He-man who is still doing all of those fabulous things to support and provide for his family.

"Grateful" doesn't begin to describe how I feel about you sharing this adventure with me. To be accepted in this highly creative world is an honor and a challenge. To have written my first book that you read and embraced is amazing and encouraging. To have written a second book that you are reading now is just awesome. I thank you. I will continue to share my journey with you and encourage you to breathe, play, and enjoy as we quilt together.

CONTENTS

Introduction 5

Quilt Projects
  GARDEN GATE 6
  GARDEN PATHWAY 10

PAPER POSIES 14
LOOSE 20
TILL THE ROWS 26
PATCH OF POSIES 32
LIMETAIL 38
LEAF DREAMS 42

BALINESE BEAUTY 46
TRIUNE 52
GARDEN GODDESSES . . 60

Resources 78
About the Author 79

Kay M. Capps Cross

INTRODUCTION

How can you portray the splendor or a garden with merely black and white? Quite simply—and therein lies the beauty. This book celebrates gardens while highlighting them against a dramatic black-and-white background. Whether a garden is water, planned, wild, or manicured, it begs to be brought indoors.

Just as gardens vary, the methods we will use to create our indoor gardens will differ. We will use easy fusible appliqué and strip piecing. Some of our gardens will employ specialty treatments and fabrics, from silk, beading, and thread painting to appliquéing hand-stitched and beaded squares from India.

While black and white is obviously my first choice in a color palette, I decided to broaden my horizons and recreate some of the designs in color. I encourage my students to venture outside the box, so I took my own advice! I hope these quilts will inspire and empower you to create an indoor wonderland all your own. I'm glad to provide the starting blocks while you cultivate your personal fabric choices and embellishments to tend and grow some fabulous quilts!

The quilt shown on the left is a tribute to my father and an interpretation of a card he made for his mother when he was small. My grandmother loved to save things and this card was carefully tucked away among her treasures. It is in amazing condition for being so old. (Sorry, Dad!) One of its most charming qualities is that my dad signed it "form Jack."

The sentiment inside the card is lovely and most likely copied straight from the blackboard at school. The cover design is what struck me the most. Its simplicity and asymmetrical balance are so like my quilts. I never guessed my design sense came "form" Jack.

Please do not feel obliged to create these gardens with the methods I use. These quilts would be stunning hand-appliquéd or painted. While I enjoy hand work, I seem to reach for it only when I need to spend a good deal of time

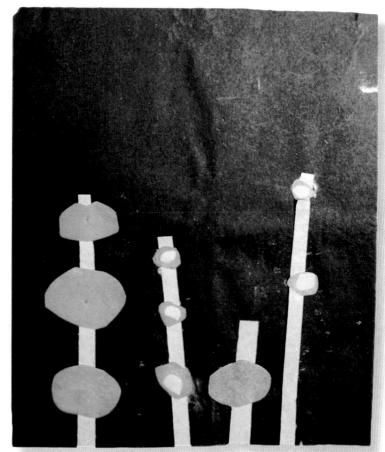

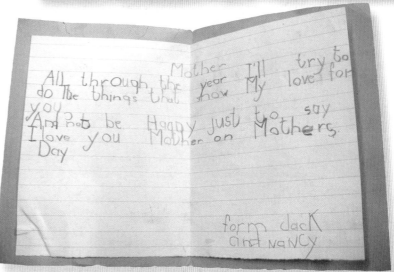

in a waiting room. Currently, life is running smoothly, so I haven't been reaching for the straw needles at all! I gladly exchange intricate hand work for speedier techniques during this engaging and exciting time of my life. My children come first, but I'll always find a way to create the quilted visions in my head.

GARDEN GATE

15½" x 23½", pieced and
quilted by the author.
*The black and lime batik fabrics
courtesy of Island Batik.*

There is something so
intriguing about a closed
garden gate. What lies beyond?
While the lure of the unknown
is intoxicating, the charm and
appeal of a gate itself is inviting.
Pause before opening and
enjoy the now—the beauty
that is the everyday. Perhaps it
will even rival the splendor that
lies beyond. This traditionally
pieced quilt celebrates
everyday beauty via high
contrast in simple patchwork.
Lime adds the intrigue. The
piecing is easy, the result is
dynamic.

FABRIC SUGGESTIONS

Small-scale polka dots with an irregular pattern create a wonderful canvas when alternated with dark and light values. A pure clear zinger color ignites the center of the quilt and adds punch between the borders. Scale changes in the border prints add interest without competing with this simple design. Try a funky print for backing.

GATHERING YOUR FABRICS

You will need five fabrics for this quilt plus backing. The yardages are based on 40" usable width of fabric.

A	Medium dark	¼ yard	white-on-black, large-scale floral print for outer border
B	Dark	¼ yard	white-on-black, medium-scale print for inner border
C	Dark	½ yard	white-on-black, small-scale print for piecing and binding
D	Light	⅛ yard	black-on-white, small-scale print for piecing
E	Lime green	¼ yard	for piecing and zinger border
Backing		⅝ yard	
Batting		19½" x 27½"	

CUTTING INSTRUCTIONS

Strips are cut across the width of the fabric unless stated otherwise.

Fabric A   2 strips 2½" wide

Fabric B   2 strips 2" wide

Fabric C   3 strips 2¼" wide (for binding)
2 strips 1½" wide
3 strips 1" wide

Fabric D   2 strips 1½" wide

Fabric E   5 strips 1" wide

SEWING INSTRUCTIONS

Make a strip-set using 3 fabric C and 3 fabric E 1" strips. Alternate their placement as shown. Press all the seam allowances in the same direction. Cut 15 segments 1½" wide from the strip-set.

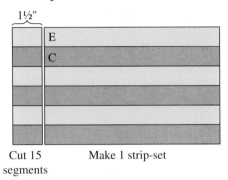

Cut 15 segments   Make 1 strip-set

Sew the segments together, turning every other segment to create the unit 1 checkerboard as shown.

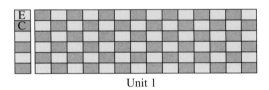

Unit 1

Make 2 strip-sets using the fabric C and fabric D 1½" strips as shown. Press the seam allowances toward the dark strip. Cut 30 segments 1½" wide from the strip-sets.

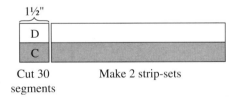

Cut 30 segments   Make 2 strip-sets

Sew 15 segments together, turning every other segment to create unit 2 checkerboards as shown. Make 2. Sew a unit 2 to each side of unit 1 and press.

Unit 2 – make 2

Make 2 strip-sets with the fabric A 2½", fabric E 1", and fabric B 2" strips as shown. Press the seams away from the E strip.

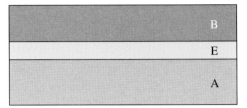

Make 2 strip-sets

Measure the width of the quilt through the center and cut 2 segments that measurement. Sew them to the sides of the quilt.

Measure the length of the quilt through the center and cut 2 segments that measurement. Sew them to the top and bottom of the quilt.

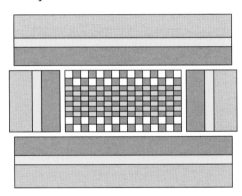

Layer the quilt top with the backing and batting, then quilt the layers by hand or machine. Trim and bind the edges with the fabric C strips.

FINISHING TOUCHES

I chose a variety of lines to quilt my black-and-white gate. The patchwork center features traditional crosshatching with a serpentine line that naturally grows into a larger crosshatch in the checkerboard rows. Sharp zigzags accentuate the darker inner border.

A tight licorice whip in the zinger border enlarges to a large licorice whip in the medium-dark border. This quilt may be small, but it is loaded with texture and pizzazz.

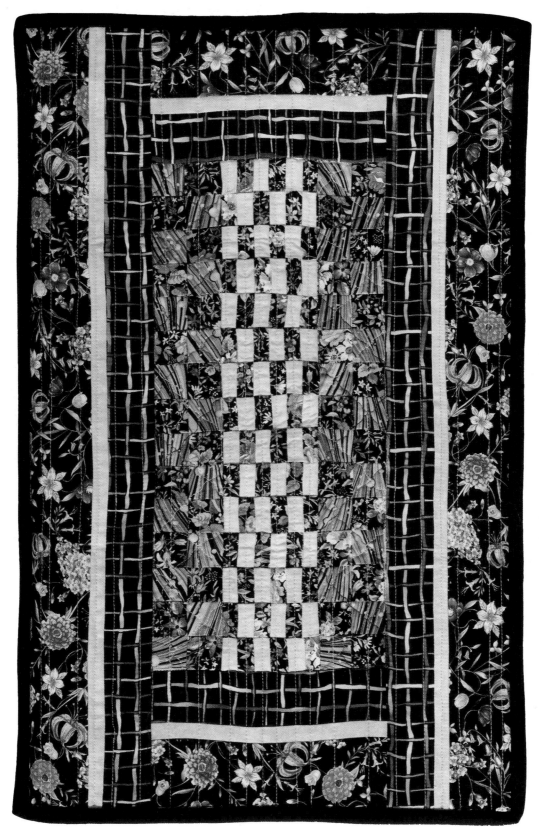

GARDEN GATE

15½" x 23½", pieced and quilted by the author

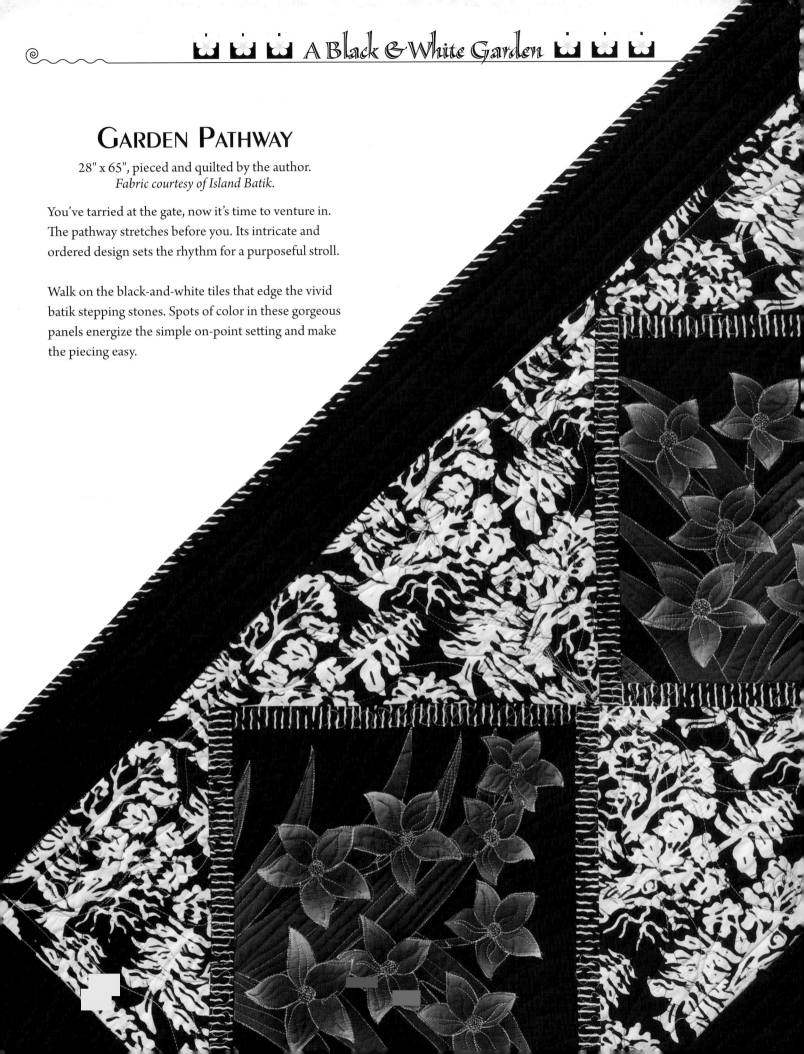

GARDEN PATHWAY

28" x 65", pieced and quilted by the author.
Fabric courtesy of Island Batik.

You've tarried at the gate, now it's time to venture in. The pathway stretches before you. Its intricate and ordered design sets the rhythm for a purposeful stroll.

Walk on the black-and-white tiles that edge the vivid batik stepping stones. Spots of color in these gorgeous panels energize the simple on-point setting and make the piecing easy.

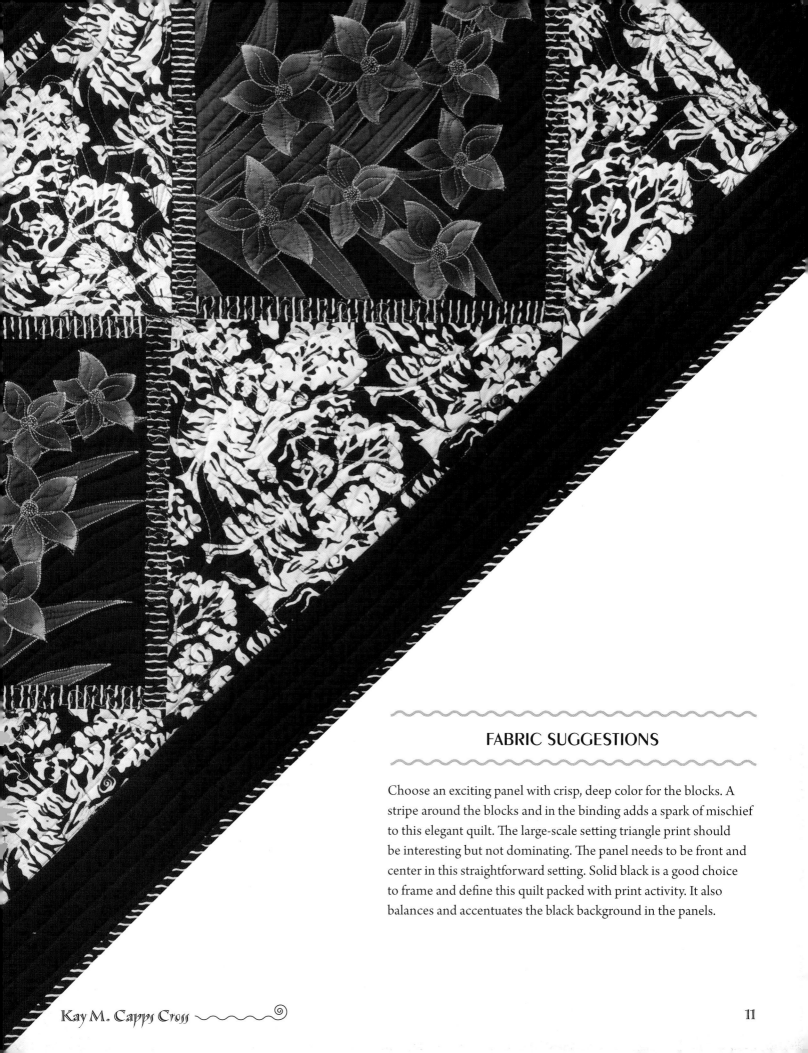

FABRIC SUGGESTIONS

Choose an exciting panel with crisp, deep color for the blocks. A stripe around the blocks and in the binding adds a spark of mischief to this elegant quilt. The large-scale setting triangle print should be interesting but not dominating. The panel needs to be front and center in this straightforward setting. Solid black is a good choice to frame and define this quilt packed with print activity. It also balances and accentuates the black background in the panels.

GATHERING YOUR FABRICS

You will need four fabrics plus backing, for this quilt. The yardages are based on 40" usable width of fabric.

A		3 panels at least 12½" square	large-scale floral batiks
B	Dark	⅞ yard	white-on-black, medium-scale stripe for framing and binding
C	Medium	1 yard	white-on-black, large-scale print for setting triangles
D	Solid black	¾ yard	for border
Backing		2⅛ yards	
Batting		36" x 73"	

CUTTING INSTRUCTIONS

Strips are cut across the width of the fabric.

Fabric A   3 squares 12½" x 12½"

Fabric B   22" square for continuous 2¼" binding
                 5 strips 1¼" wide cut into
                     6 rectangles 1¼" x 12½"
                     6 rectangles 1¼" x 14"

Fabric C   1 square 22" cut twice on the diagonal
                 2 squares 12" cut once on the diagonal

Fabric D   5 strips 4" wide

SEWING INSTRUCTIONS

You will be highlighting the panels by framing them with the B fabric.

Sew the 12½" long fabric B rectangles to opposite sides of the 3 A panels. Press the seams away from the panels.

Sew the 14" long fabric B rectangles to the remaining sides of the panels. Press as before.

Join the framed panels with the fabric C setting triangles into rows and join the rows as shown.

The setting and corner triangle are cut generously to completely surround the blocks. The corners of the blocks will float and not meet the border.

Join the fabric D strips end-to-end with diagonal seams.

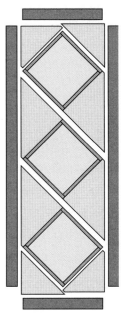

Measure the length of the quilt through the center and cut 2 fabric D strips to that measurement. Add to the sides of the quilt and press the seam allowances toward the border.

Measure the width of the quilt through the center and cut 2 fabric D strips to that measurement. Add to the ends of the quilt and press the seam allowances toward the border.

Layer the quilt top with the backing and batting, then quilt the layers by hand or machine.

Make continuous binding from the 22" square and bind the edges of the quilt.

FINISHING TOUCHES

I had great fun quilting swirly leaves in the setting triangles. You can barely see them since the print is so busy, but I know they are there. I also tucked some leaves in the top left and bottom right corners. They are a surprise in the straight line quilting of the border.

I didn't want to get in the way of the beauty of the panels, so I merely outlined the blossoms and added a bit of shadow quilting for texture. Quilted licorice whips define the striped frame.

Let the panels determine the style and density of the quilting you choose.

GARDEN PATHWAY

28" x 65", pieced and quilted by the author. *Batik fabric courtesy of Bali Fabric, Inc.*

An exquisite hand-beaded square from India adds richness and depth to this GARDEN PATHWAY. Beading and embellishments are fun to experiment with but are time-consuming. Utilizing a handcrafted panel provides an alternative and celebrates Indian artistry at the same time.

The quilting is similar to the black-and-white version. It is much more visible and adds to the elegant and highly decorative style of this piece.

13

PAPER POSIES

29½" x 33", pieced and quilted by the author

Every journey ends, but with the end comes a cache of memories to carry with us always. PAPER POSIES provide a tangible sliver of garden splendor to keep throughout the long winter months.

Tissue paper crackles and crunches as it's manipulated into a memory that will fit in a vase. Not exact, but the impression transports us to the rhythm and sights of a garden stroll.

Kay M. Capps Cross

Deanne Rogers

FABRIC SUGGESTIONS

Crisp black-and-white prints evoke the pungent smells of freshly turned soil ready to be sown with color. Vary the prints, values, and scales for the most interest. The smallest bit of a clear, vibrant yellow adds the punch needed for a smashing quilt.

GATHERING YOUR FABRICS

You will need seven fabrics for the quilt plus backing and a variety of scraps or fat eighths for the posies. The yardages are based on 40" usable width of fabric.

A	Dark	½ yard	solid black pin-tucked for outer border
B	Medium	¼ yard	white-on-black, medium-scale exploded weave print for middle border
C	Medium light	⅛ yard	black-on-white, small-scale geometric print for inner border
D	Light	⅝ yard	black-on-white, large-scale leaf print for quilt center
E	Intense yellow	⅛ yard	for cornerstones and posy centers
F	Dark	½ yard	black-on-black square print for stem and bias-cut binding
G	Dark	¼ yard	white-on-black small-scale polka dot for vase
H	Scraps	¼ yard total	black-and-white prints of different values and scales for the posies
Backing		1⅛ yard	
Batting		34" x 37"	
Paper-backed fusible web		1½ yards of 12" wide	

CUTTING INSTRUCTIONS

Strips are cut across the width of the fabric unless stated otherwise.

Fabric A   4 strips 4" wide cut into 2 strips 4" x 29½" and 2 strips 4" x 26"

Fabric B   3 strips 2" wide cut into 2 strips 2" x 23" and 2 strips 2" x 19½"
1 strip 2" wide cut into 2 strips 2" x 19½"

Fabric C   2 strips 1½" wide cut into 2 strips 1½" x 21" and 2 strips 1½" x 17½"

CUTTING INSTRUCTIONS (CONT.)

Fabric D   1 strip 17½" wide cut into 1 rectangle 17½" x 21"

Fabric E   1 strip 2" wide cut into 4 squares 2" x 2" then trim to 1½" wide
and cut 4 squares 1½" x 1½"

Fabric F   1 square 17" x 17" for 2¼" continuous binding

SEWING INSTRUCTIONS

You will be adding two borders with cornerstones and one final textured border to the quilt center.

Sew the fabric C 1½" x 21" strips to the sides of the fabric D rectangle. Press the seams out towards the strips.

Sew the fabric E 1½" cornerstones to the ends of the fabric C 1½" x 17½" strips and press the seams toward the strips. Add to the top and bottom and press the seams outward. In the same way, sew the fabric B 2" x 23" strips to the sides. Add the 2" cornerstones to the ends of the fabric B 2" x 19½" strips, then add them to the top and bottom. Press.

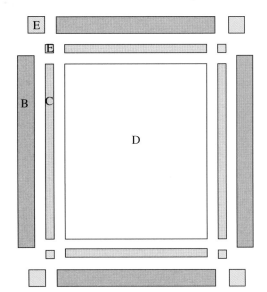

Sew the fabric C 4" x 26" strips to the sides of the quilt and fabric C 4" x 29½" strips to the top and bottom. Press the seams outward.

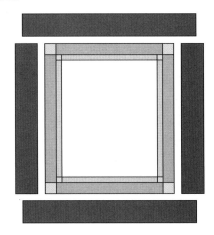

Trace the already reversed blossoms, centers, stems, and vase parts (pages 18–19) on paper-backed fusible web. Trace 5 each posy centers and templates #1, #2, and #3. Trace 4 of posy template #4 and 3 of posy template #5. *Vary the lines a bit from one copy to another to make each flower unique.*

Cut the pieces ⅛" beyond the traced line. Cut out the centers of the vase and larger posy parts about ½" inside the traced line to reduce bulk when layering.

Place the fusible web posies on the wrong side of an assortment of the fabric H posy scraps and follow the manufacturer's directions to fuse.

Place the fusible web centers on the wrong side of fabric E and fuse.

Place the fusible web stem on the wrong side of fabric F and fuse.

Cut out all the pieces exactly on the traced lines.

Select 3, 4, and 5 posy pieces with center pieces for each of 5 flowers.

Peel the paper off of all but the bottom layer of each posy part and stack the layers. Lightly press each posy to hold the pieces together.

Refer to the quilt photo to arrange the vase, vase lip, stem, and posies. Tuck the bottom of the stem under the top layer of the vase between it and the vase lip. Tuck the tops of the stems under the posies. Remove the paper from all the pieces and fuse in place.

With yellow thread, highlight the center of the posies with a bit of stitching through all layers.

Spruce up the vase with some decorative stitching.

Layer the quilt top with the backing and batting, then quilt the layers by hand or machine.

Make continuous binding from the fabric F 17" square and bind the edges of the quilt.

FINISHING TOUCHES

The vase and posies are the stars of this quilt, so I quilted white vertical lines to texturize yet not emphasize the background. I let the inner border plump by only stitching in the ditch on either side of it. The middle border has irregular black zigzags that take us right out to the pin-tucked border. It looks like crosshatch quilting, and I didn't have to do any of it! I added complementary straight lines in black to highlight the crosshatch look.

I continued the flow of the decorative stitches in the vase by stitching almost parallel black lines at uneven intervals throughout the vase. I simply outlined all of the posy layers, staying away from the bright center. I didn't want the black thread to mute the yellow sparkle.

PAPER POSIES

29½" x 33", pieced and quilted by the author.
Fabric courtesy of Bali Fabric, Inc.

The surprising chartreuse flannel background underscores the striking burnt umber flannel vase and allows the vivid blue and purple flannel posies to dominate the quilted still life. The posies are a layered combination of flannel, corduroy, and silk in hues ranging from deep purple to turquoise. The inner and middle borders gradually lead the eye to the dark blue with purple corduroy border. Multiple types of fabric underline and amplify the rich coloration in this quilt. Be bold and take a chance on your own quilted memories.

PAPER POSIES
Templates

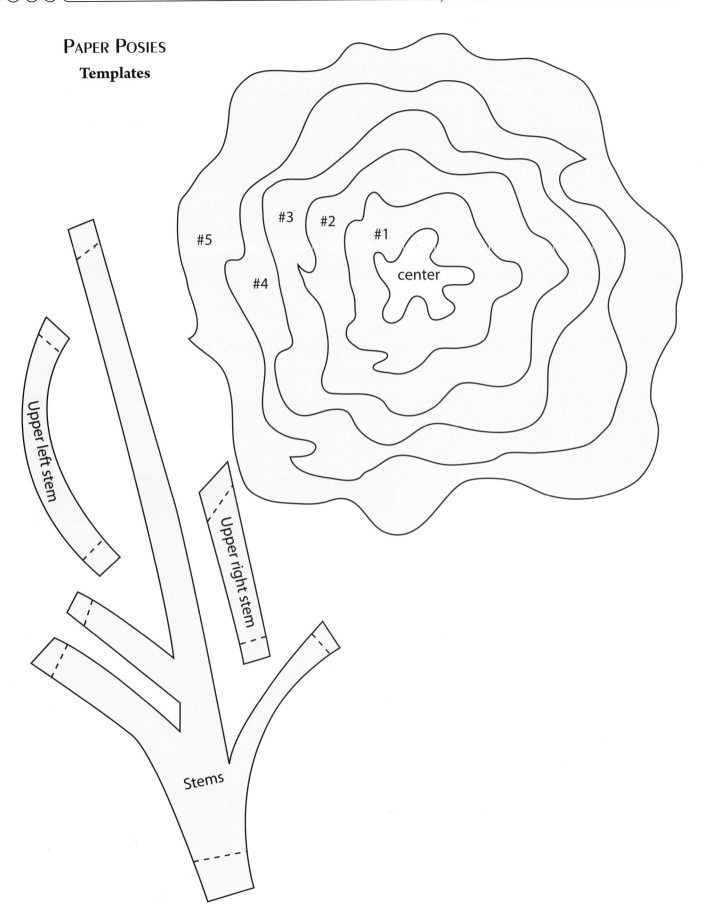

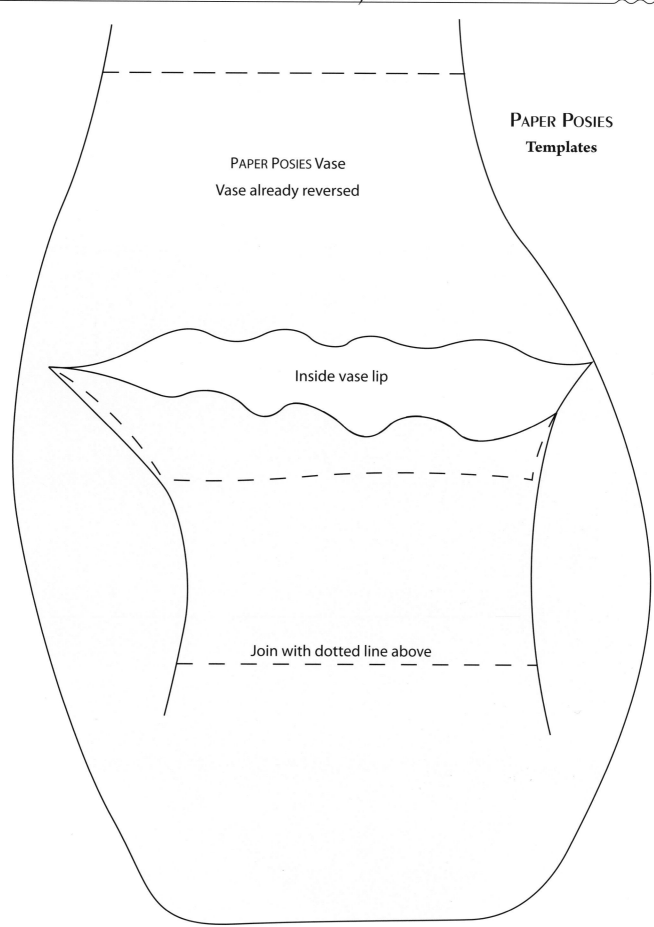

PAPER POSIES

Templates

PAPER POSIES Vase

Vase already reversed

Inside vase lip

Join with dotted line above

LoosE

18" x 59", pieced and quilted by the author.
Fabrics courtesy of Island Batik.

Hovering above the cattails, the dragonflies dance
and play. Their precarious existence depends on the
length of Mr. Frog's tongue among other threats. The
starkness of this reality is shown in their amorphous
fluttering against the dark and intricate layering of the
background. My dear friend, Lucy, inspired this quilt
with her love of dragonflies and her quest to teach us
that dragonflies do not have antennae. I for one have
learned and will remember.

FABRIC SUGGESTIONS

Choose three black-and-white prints that vary greatly in scale, from medium to dark, to add movement to the pieced background. There is no need to try to keep the prints too close together, since this does not have a watercolor feel to it. It can be chunkier in the fabric changes. Choose vibrant lime green batik in a variety of patterns for the dragonflies. The bigger the differences in scale without changing value too much, the better. You will be cutting background and binding strips from the same fabrics.

GATHERING YOUR FABRICS

You will need six fabrics for this quilt plus backing. The yardages are based on 40" usable width of fabric.

A	Medium	⅔ yard	white-on-black large-scale floral batik
B	Medium dark	⅔ yard	white-on-black medium-scale burst batik
C	Dark	⅔ yard	white-on-black small-scale dotted batik
D	3 Medium lime batiks	⅙ yard each	
Backing		1⅞ yard	
Batting		26" x 67"	
Paper-backed fusible web		1 yard	

CUTTING INSTRUCTIONS

All strips are cut across width of fabric unless otherwise stated. Binding is made from the 2¼" strips.

Fabrics A, B, & C—cut from all 3 fabrics

2 strips 1" wide (total of 6)	1 strip 1½" wide (total of 3)
2 strips 2" wide (total of 6)	2 strips 2¼" wide (total of 6)
1 strip 2½" wide (total of 3)	1 strip 3" wide (total of 3)

Set aside any four 2¼" strips for the binding.

Cut all the 1" strips in random lengths, from 4" to the full length of the strip. Sew all the pieces together end-to-end to make one long 1" wide strip. Do not deliberate on strip placement or work to make a pattern. Just grab and sew.

Repeat for all the other strips, working with one width at a time.

Cut from the long strips

1" strips — 3 strips 1" x 56½"

1½" strips — 1 strip 1½" x 56½"
 1 strip 1½" x 59½"

2" strips — 2 strips 2" x 55½"
 2 strips 2" x 56½"

2¼" strips — 1 strip 2¼" x 42"

2½" strips — 1 strip 2½" x 59½"
 1 strip 2½" x 56½"

3" strips — 1 strip 3" x 59½"

Stitch the 2" x 55½" strips together lengthwise. Press the seam allowance to one side.

Sew the 59½" strips together in the following order: 3", 1½", 2½". Press the seam allowances to one side and add the strip-set to the right side of the 55½" section, aligning the top edges.

Sew the 56½" strips together in the following order: 1", 2", 1", 2½", 2", 1", 1½". Press the seam allowances to one side and add to the previous set, aligning the top edges.

Add the 2¼" x 42" strip, aligning the top edges. Press the seam allowance to one side.

2" 2"   3" 1½" 2½"   1" 2" 1" 2½" 2" 1" 1½"   2¼"

ADDING THE DRAGONFLIES

Enlarge and trace 3 sets of the already reversed dragonfly parts on paper-backed fusible web. Cut out ⅛" outside the traced line.

Place the fusible-web dragonfly parts on the wrong side of the C fabrics and follow the manufacturer's directions to fuse.

Cut out the dragonfly parts exactly on the traced line.

Peel the paper from the back of the dragonflies and arrange them on the background using the quilt photo for reference.

Fuse the dragonflies in place.

FINISHING THE QUILT

Layer the quilt top with the backing and batting and quilt by hand or machine.

To accentuate the chunky strip background, I treated some of the strips individually for quilting. I used a variety of quilting motifs to accomplish this including serpentine stitch, zigzags, small and large licorice whips, short horizontal lines, and loops.

I quilted right over the dragonflies to add detailing to the wings and bodies. This also secures them to the quilt. I don't depend on the fusing to hold them; I stitch them down during the quilting process.

Join the set-aside 2¼" binding strips end-to-end in one long strip for binding and bind the edges of the quilt.

Remember to sign your artwork!

LOOSE
Templates

Enlarge 200%

Kay M. Capps Cross

LOOSE

18" x 58", pieced and quilted by the author.
Fabrics courtesy of Bali Fabrics, Inc.

The background has been simplified with a playful wholecloth flannel for this version of LoosE. The quilting correlates with this lighthearted interpretation by being delightfully simple. I had such a grand time quilting this piece. I envisioned fairies riding the dragonflies and giggling as they flew. Their toes left fairy flight patterns in the quilting. You can't see the fairies, but you know they were there by the curlicue wisps left under the dragonfly wings. Buoyant and whimsical, the fairy flight quilting is a counterpoint to the straight quilted lines above the dragonflies. Order in the universe I suppose—but oh, what fun to watch the fairies fly!

TILL THE ROWS

54½" x 63½", pieced and quilted by the author. *Fabrics courtesy of Telegraph Road Studio.*

Not so far from the meadow, a tilled field is brimming with life. The charming irregularity of the 15-patch block provides rows to till and rows to plant. Lush green vines flourish in their well-tended ranks. This crop basically grows itself. A bit of easy piecing with bias vines and fusible appliqué provides the perfect growing conditions for a spectacular quilt.

Kay M. Capps Cross

FABRIC SUGGESTIONS

Select a very dark and rich black for the rows. There is a jump in value to the medium dark and medium print of the 15-patch blocks. The binding is a repeat of the dark vine print used in the rows. Choose vine fabrics with color variations and a defined print for veining on the leaves.

GATHERING YOUR FABRICS

You will need five fabrics for this quilt plus backing fabric and a variety of greens for the leaves. The yardages are based on 40" usable width of fabric.

A	Dark	2½ yards	black-on-black, small-scale vine print for rows and binding
B	Medium dark	1¼ yards	grey-on-black, large-scale swirl print
C	Medium	1 1/8 yards	black-on-white, medium-scale dense squiggle print
D	Medium green	1¼ yards	small-scale textured print
E	Medium light green	2 yards	yellow-green large-scale brush stroke print
Backing		3½ yards	
Batting		62½" x 71½"	
Paper-backed fusible web		5 yards of 12" wide	

CUTTING INSTRUCTIONS

Strips are cut across the width of the fabric unless stated otherwise.

Fabric A   5 strips 6½" x 63½" cut lenghwise
             1 square 25" x 25" for continuous 2¼" binding

Fabric B   6 strips 2" wide
             6 strips 3" wide
             4 strips 2½" wide

Fabric C   6 strips 2½"
             4 strips 2"
             4 strips 3"

Fabric D   1 square 22" x 22" for 1¼" continuous-bias vine

SEWING INSTRUCTIONS

Making the Blocks

Make 6 strip-sets using fabric B 2" and 3" strips and fabric C 2½" strips as shown. Press the seam allowances toward the outer strips.

From the strip-sets, cut 28 segments 1½" wide, 28 segments 2¼" wide, and 28 segments 3¼" wide.

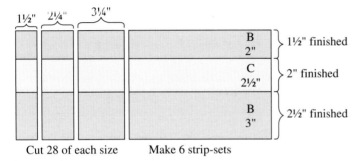

Cut 28 of each size   Make 6 strip-sets

Make 4 strip-sets using fabric C 2" and 3" strips and fabric B 2½" strips as shown. Press the seam allowances in toward the center strip.

From the strip sets, cut 28 segments 2" wide and 28 segments 2½" wide.

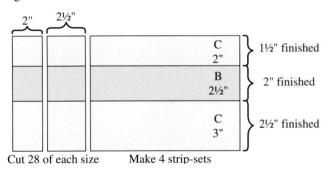

Cut 28 of each size   Make 4 strip-sets

Arrange the segments from narrowest to widest and join to make a 15-patch block. Make 28.

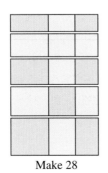

Make 28

Making the Rows

Arrange the blocks in 4 vertical rows of 7 blocks each, orienting the blocks as shown, and sew the rows.

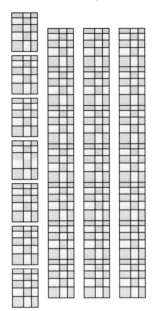

Measure the length of the block rows. Trim if necessary so they are all 63½" in length.

Join the strips and block rows as shown. Press the seam allowances toward the strips.

Adding the Vines

Make 1¼" continuous bias from the fabric D 22" square.

Fold the strip in half lengthwise, wrong sides together, and press the strip carefully without stretching.

Hang the quilt on a design wall and arrange the bias vine in gentle curves in each row as shown in the quilt photo.

Mark the stem curve on the quilt and pin the stems in place, easing in fullness. Stitch the stem to the quilt ¼" in from the raw edges.

Fold the stem back over the seam and gently press, easing in fullness. Machine stitch the stem down with invisible thread.

Making the Leaves

Trace 54 leaves on paper-backed fusible web following the numbers indicated on the templates (pages 30–31). You will trace them as they appear and in reverse for a total of 54 leaves. Cut the leaves out ⅛" beyond the traced line.

Cut the center of the leaves out ½" inside the traced line to maintain flexibility after fusing.

Hint: Trace the larger leaves first, then trace the smaller leaves on the pieces cut out of the centers of the larger leaves.

Place the fusible web leaves on the wrong side of the green fabrics and follow the manufacturer's directions to fuse. Refer to the quilt photo to add the leaves to the stem and fuse in place.

Layer the quilt top with the backing and batting, then quilt the layers by hand or machine.

Make continuous binding from the fabric A 25" square and bind the edges of the quilt.

FINISHING TOUCHES

I quilted the leaves down with a variegated green thread to add veining. I switched to black thread to echo quilt around the leaves. I wanted to draw out the leaves and not interfere with the simple vigor of the vine. Busy quilting would have pulled focus and diluted the strength of the rows.

TILL THE ROWS
40" x 35", pieced and quilted
by the author

This rich color version utilizes plum philodendron leaves on a burnt orange canvas to illustrate what houseplants would look like if they had a choice. The echo quilting unifies the background and allows the vine to grow right off the quilt.

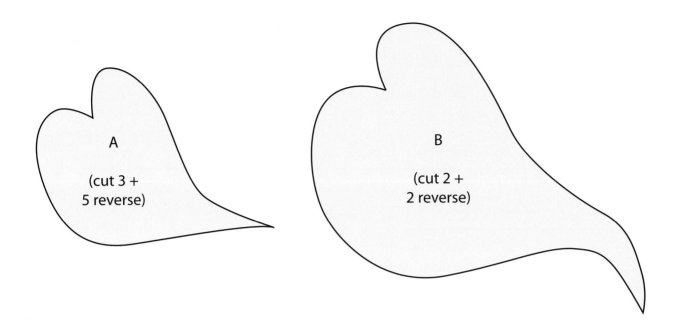

A

(cut 3 +
5 reverse)

B

(cut 2 +
2 reverse)

TILL THE ROWS

Templates

Enlarge 200%

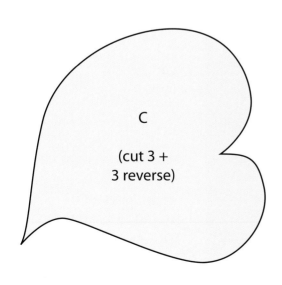

C

(cut 3 +
3 reverse)

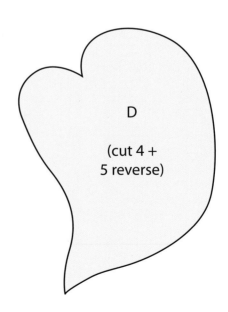

D

(cut 4 +
5 reverse)

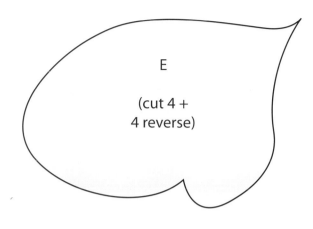

E

(cut 4 +
4 reverse)

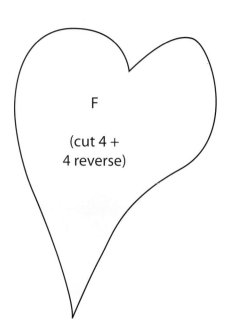

F

(cut 4 +
4 reverse)

TILL THE ROWS
Templates

Enlarge 200%

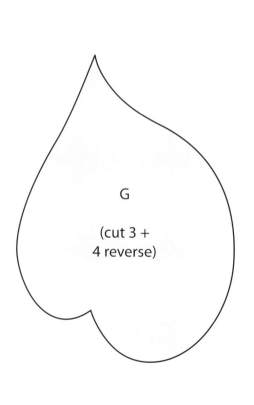

G

(cut 3 +
4 reverse)

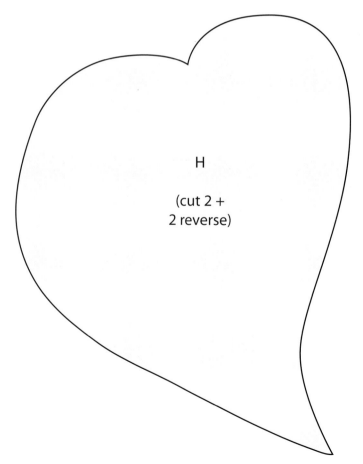

H

(cut 2 +
2 reverse)

PATCH OF POSIES

54½" x 63½", pieced and quilted by the author. *White print fabrics courtesy of Telegraph Road Studio.*

The scattered wildflowers at the edge of the backyard frolic and play next to the ordered beauty of the garden. Young and old blooms mingle and enjoy their freedom as they sprinkle the meadow with color.

Quickly create your own wildflower sanctuary with fusible appliqué posies sprinkled on a pieced field. The 15-patch blocks provide a bit of structure to support the wind-blown posies as they grow.

 Kay M. Capps Cross

FABRIC SUGGESTIONS

Choose prints that vary greatly in scale, yet are of the same value. This creates doubt that this quilt is pieced. Appearing to be wholecloth, on closer scrutiny the quilt will reveal that there are three fabrics expertly matched and pieced to create the background.

Hand-dyed fabrics give a smooth almost suede appearance to the wildflowers. Choose pieces with enough variety in value to shade and shadow the posies. You could substitute batik with value differences but avoid a flat or single-value fabric that will hinder movement. You want to allow the posies to pop.

The binding should be very close in value to the prints but ever so slightly darker. This provides a short rest before your eye continues outward in search of more meadow. Allow the posies to waft by not using too dark a print that will halt the journey and hem in the wildflowers.

GATHERING YOUR FABRICS

You will need six fabrics for this quilt plus backing and binding. The yardages are based on 40" usable width of fabric.

A	Medium light	1⅔ yards	black-on-white, large-scale paisley print
B	Medium light	1½ yards	black-on-white, small-scale crackle print
C	Medium light	1¼ yards	black-on-white, large-scale swirl print
D	Medium	¾ yard	red/coral hand dyed for posies
E	Medium	¾ yard	red/orange hand dyed for posies
F	Medium light	⅛ yard	yellow hand dyed for posy centers
Backing		3½ yards	black-on-white print
Binding		¾ yard	black-on-white, medium-scale swirl for binding
Batting		62½" x 71½"	
Paper-backed fusible web		4½ yards, 12" wide	

CUTTING INSTRUCTIONS

Strips are cut across the width of the fabric unless stated otherwise.

Fabric A	8 strips 6½" wide cut into 31 strips 6½" x 9½"
Fabric B	6 strips 2" wide 6 strips 3" wide 4 strips 2½" wide
Fabric C	6 strips 2½" wide 4 strips 2" wide 4 strips 3" wide
Binding	1 square 25" x 25" for 2¼" continuous-bias binding

SEWING INSTRUCTIONS

Sewing the Background

Make 6 strip-sets using fabric B 2" and 3" strips and fabric C 2½" strips as shown. Press the seam allowances toward the outer strips.

From the strip-sets, cut 32 segments 1½" wide, 32 segments 2¼" wide, and 32 segments 3 ¼" wide.

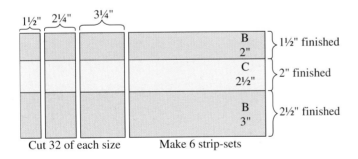

Cut 32 of each size   Make 6 strip-sets

Make 4 strip-sets using fabric C 2" and 3" strips and fabric B 2½" strips as shown. Press the seam allowances in toward the center strip.

From the strip-sets, cut 32 segments 2" wide and 32 segments 2½" wide.

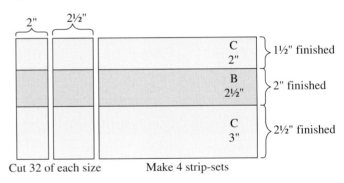

Cut 32 of each size   Make 4 strip-sets

Arrange the segments from narrowest to widest and join to make a 15-patch block. Make 32.

Make 32

Lay out 7 rows of 15-patch blocks and fabric A strips in a checkerboard arrangement as shown, with a total of 9 blocks and strips in each row. Sew the rows together, pressing the seam allowances toward fabric A. Join the rows.

Making the Posies

Trace 20 of each piece of the already reversed three-piece posies on paper-backed fusible web for a total of 60 flowers (see page 36). Cut out ⅛" beyond the traced line.

Hint: Cut out the center of the largest posy pieces ½" inside the traced line and use it for tracing the posy centers.

Place the fusible web petal pieces on the wrong side of fabrics D and E and the posy centers on the wrong side of fabric F. Fuse following the manufacturer's instructions.

Cut out the posies and posy centers exactly on the traced line. Peel the paper off of the posies parts and centers.

Stack the three pieces for each posy. Play around with the pieces to get the value differences in the layers.

Referring to the quilt photo, lay out the posies on the pieced meadow. When you are pleased with the arrangement, fuse the posies in place according to manufacturer's directions.

Layer the quilt top with the backing and batting, then quilt the layers by hand or machine.

Make continuous binding from the 25" square and bind the edges of the quilt.

FINISHING TOUCHES

The posies are permanently secured by the quilting process. Use a coordinating thread to quilt texture and depth into the blossoms.

Use white thread on the background to define and elongate the meadow with straight vertical quilting.

The texturized posy centers pull the flowers right up off of the simple yet interesting background. Variegated thread adds even more depth to the ruffly petals.

PATCH OF POSIES
Template
more on page 36

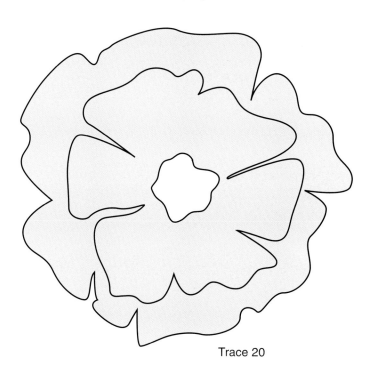

Trace 20

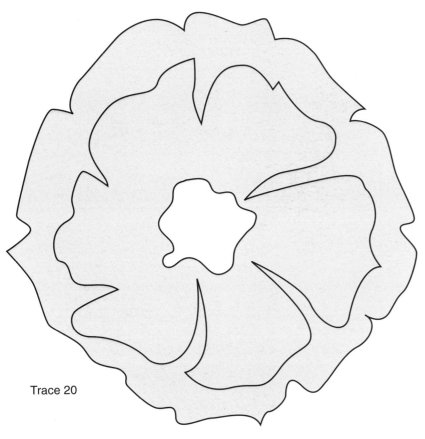

Trace 20

PATCH OF POSIES

Templates

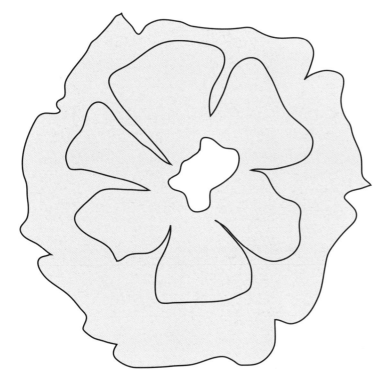

Trace 20

PATCH OF POSIES

30½" x 27½", pieced and
quilted by the author

The soft, velvety hand-dyed
cotton posies infused with color
plunge us into the rich, earthy
smells and sights of the heat of
summer. Lush and full, the fabric
choices completely change the
look and feel of this version.
The prints mixed with a suede-
looking solid provide wonderful
textural interest.

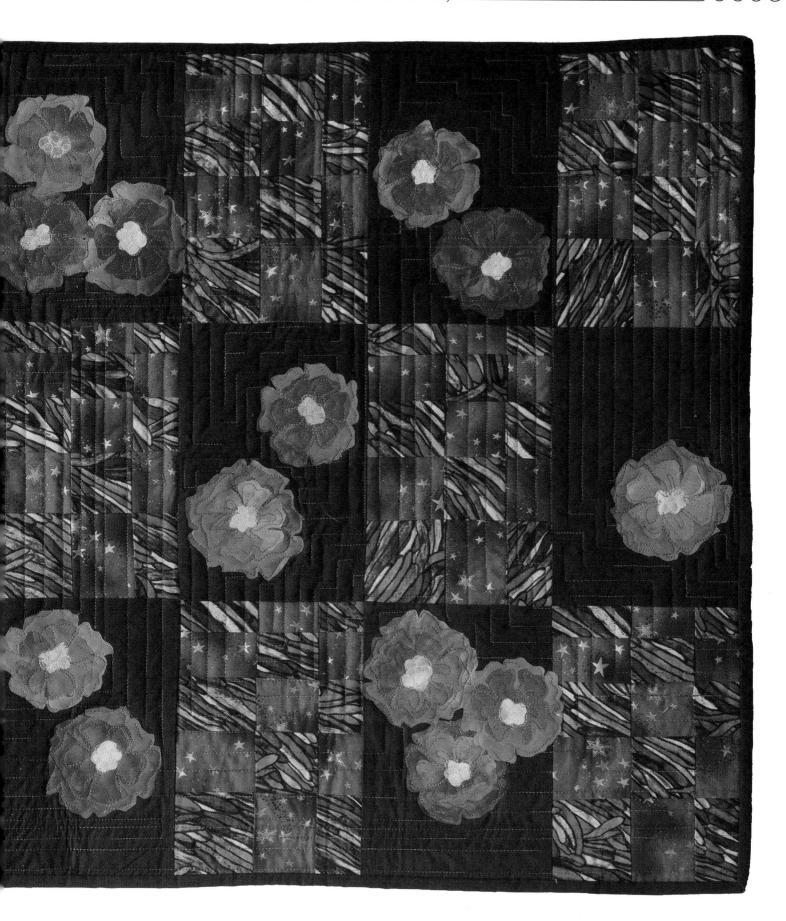

LIMETAIL

15½" x 12½", pieced and quilted by the author. *Fabric courtesy of Island Batik.*

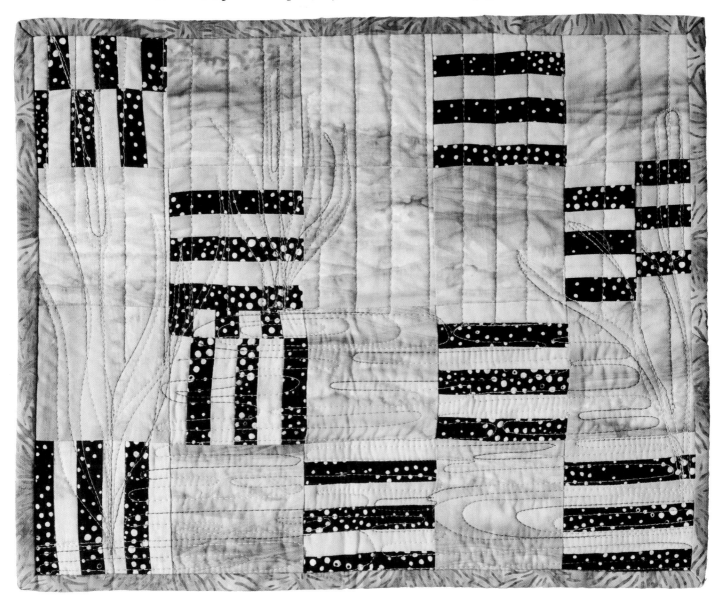

At the side of a pond, the cattails hold court. Their story is thread "painted" on a pieced background and brought to life through the quilting. Quietly standing watch, the cattails exemplify peace and tranquility amid the bustle of pond life.

FABRIC SUGGESTIONS

Choose batik with subtle yet noticeable variations in coloration and value. Using too "flat" a batik will reduce the movement and shading. Choose a dark black that will provide contrast and interest in the incidental black stripes. The binding should be a darker value than the background lime to provide a frame for the LIMETAIL story. Choosing one with a pattern will also add texture and accent the punctuation mark that the binding provides.

GATHERING YOUR FABRICS

You will need only two fabrics for this quilt plus backing and binding. The yardages are based on 40" usable width of fabric.

A	Dark	⅛ yard	white-on-black, small-scale poka dot
B	Medium	¼ yard	lime batik
Binding		⅓ yard	
Backing		⅔ yard or a fat quarter	
Batting		19½" x 16½"	

CUTTING INSTRUCTIONS

All strips are cut across width of fabric.

Fabric A	3 strips 1" wide
Fabric B	3 strips 1" wide
	1 strip 3½" wide cut into 11 squares 3½" x 3½"
Binding	4 strips 2¼" wide, cut on the bias

SEWING INSTRUCTIONS

Make a strip-set with the 1" strips, alternating their placement as shown. Press the seam allowance toward the darker strip.

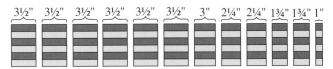

From the strip-set, cut
6 segments 3½"
1 segment 3"
2 segments 2¼"
2 segments 1¾"
1 segment 1"

Make a block with the 3" and 1" segments and make 2 blocks with the 2¼" and 1¾" segments, reversing the placement of the segments as shown. Press the seam allowances to one side.

Make 1   Make 1   Make 1

Arrange the blocks in 4 rows of 5. Sew the blocks into rows and join the rows.

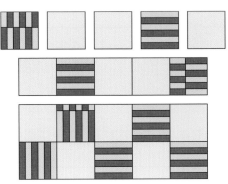

Use the cattail shapes (page 41) to mark your quilt top for quilting. They are reversed for appliqué, so remember that when you are marking for quilting.

Layer the quilt top with the backing and batting, then quilt the layers by hand or machine, outlining the cattails.

I quilted water pooling and moving around the stems. The atmosphere above the water is quilted in straight vertical lines to contrast with the horizontal water movement.

Join the 2¼" binding strips end-to-end with a diagonal seam. Press the seams open, then press the strip lengthwise, wrong sides together. Bind the edges of the quilt.

LIMETAIL

15½" x 12½",
pieced and quilted by the author

Another version of LIMETAIL employs a contemporary fabric as a 15½" x 12½" wholecloth backdrop for batik cattails. The strength of the background changes the balance of the quilt.

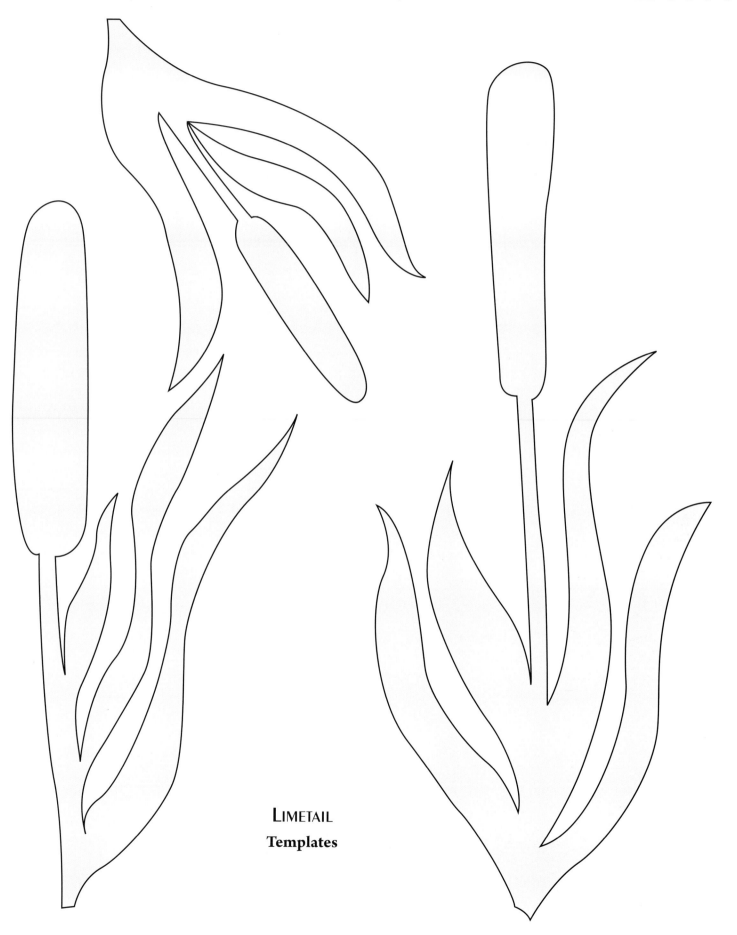

LIMETAIL

Templates

LEAF DREAMS

17½" x 29½", pieced and quilted
by the author. *Fabrics courtesy
of Bali Fabrics, Inc.*

Silk and stalks—pure, simple, and
strong. Not a leaf is in sight, nor is
one needed. This quilt has clean,
uncomplicated, and beautiful lines.
However, LEAF DREAMS represents
yearning for what we don't have, even
when we don't need it.

Naked stalks long to be dressed in
foliage. Surrounding the flowers, the
background fabric represents their
"leaf dreams" with its beautiful foliage
design. Made with rectangular yo-yos
and "almost ruching," the flower heads
glisten with beaded tears.

FABRIC SUGGESTIONS

Choose a patchwork print batik that implies piecing. The illusion doesn't make you lazy, it makes you clever! The foliage print background is a smaller scale that differentiates it from the border. Silk for the stems adds sheen and liquidity. The cotton blossoms have an interesting crispness that the silk versions lack. Be sure to choose batik with wide color variation to shade the blossoms, or choose two separate fabrics for greater value differences. For maximum shading and beauty, use a light center with a darker posy or reverse the values. The darkest value in the quilt is in the binding that contains and defines the design.

GATHERING YOUR FABRICS

You will need a minimum of four fabrics for this quilt plus backing and binding. The yardages are based on 40" usable width of fabric.

A	Medium dark	⅜ yard	white-on-black, large-scale patchwork print for outer border
B	Medium	⅜ yard	white-on-black, medium-scale foliage print for background
C	Dark	½ yard	rusty brown silk for stems
D	Vibrant	½ yard	orange/gold batik
Backing		¾ yard	
Batting		21½" x 33½"	
Binding		½ yard	dark white-on-black, medium-scale swirl print, bias-cut binding

* Additional Supplies — Assorted beads for embellishing

CUTTING INSTRUCTIONS

All strips are cut across width of fabric unless otherwise stated. Binding strips are cut on the bias.

Fabric A   3 strips 3½" wide cut into
                   2 strips 3½" x 29½"
                   2 strips 3½" x 11½"

Fabric B   1 strip 11½" wide cut into
                   a rectangle 11½" x 23½"

CUTTING INSTRUCTIONS (CONT.)

Fabric C   1 strip 13½" wide cut into
      3 bias strips 1¼" as shown

Fabric D   1 strip 9" wide cut into
      3 rectangles 9" x 11"
      1 strip 5" wide cut into
      3 rectangles 5" x 6"

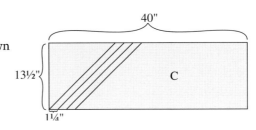

SEWING INSTRUCTIONS

Sew the shorter fabric A strips to the top and bottom of the fabric B rectangle. Press the seams out towards the strips.

Sew the longer fabric A strips to the sides. Press.

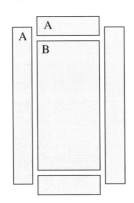

Fold the fabric C bias strips, in half lengthwise with wrong sides together and press. Cut 3 segments of 10", 14", and 17".

Referring to the figure below, arrange the 14" segment in the center position. Sew in place ¼" from the raw edge.

Fold over, press, and sew the folded edge in place using matching or invisible thread.

Next, place the 10" segment in the lower position and sew in place as before.

Repeat with the 17" stem. Make sure it covers the ends of the other two stems.

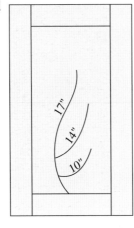

Layer the quilt top with the backing and batting. Echo quilt around the stems and add texture to the patchwork border with straight lines.

Making the Posies

To make the yo-yo posies, fold the edges of a fabric D rectangle over about ¼" and hand baste around the 4 edges. Pull up the basting thread, tightening the gathers to make the blossom. Repeat with the 5 remaining fabric D 9" x 11" and 5" x 6" rectangles.

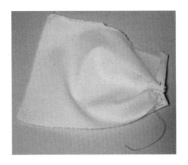

Center a smaller yo-yo on a larger yo-yo. Join them at the center and knot the thread but do not cut it yet. Use the thread to free-form ruche or plait the yo-yos to texture and create fullness. You do not need to create individual petals; merely crinkle and gather in the edges.

Continue until the posy has the size and texture you want. The more stitches you take, the smaller and stiffer the posy will become.

Embellishing the Posies

Add sparkle to the posies with embellishments One option is to use a larger bead with a smaller seed bead to secure it. Bring a knotted, double threaded needle up through the posy in the desired position. String the beads onto the needle. Bypass the seed bead and take the needle back through the center of the large bead. Continue down through the posy, tighten the thread, and knot.

To create beaded stamen "tears," select a large bead for the base, a bugle bead, and a seed bead. Bring a knotted, double threaded needle up through the posy in the desired position. String the beads onto the needle in the order listed. Bypass the seed bead and take the needle back through the bugle and large beads. Continue down through the posy, tighten the thread, and knot. Bugle beads can have sharp edges so always put a bead on either side to prevent thread breakage.

Choose a specialty bead and stack 4 seed beads on top of it. Bring a knotted, double threaded needle up through the posy in the desired position. String the stack of beads onto the needle in the order listed. Bypass the top seed bead and thread back through the center of the stack. Continue down through the posy, tighten the thread, and knot. Stitch the blossoms to the quilt.

LEAF DREAMS
17½" x 29½", pieced and quilted by the author.
Fabrics courtesy of Bali Fabrics, Inc.

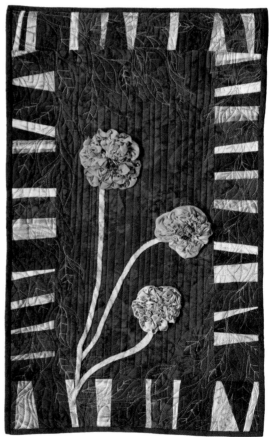

This royal version utilizes only 4 yo-yos for the blossoms. Two of them are single layered and rely more heavily on beading to add dimension.

BALINESE BEAUTY

18" x 32½", pieced and quilted by the author. *Batik fabric courtesy of Bali Fabrics, Inc.*

I adore the stark simplicity of a single-stemmed beauty. This blossom was designed to honor the pure beauty of the batiks of Bali with their intense color and clarity. This design is easily accomplished with fusible appliqué. Now that is simple beauty! While I embrace stress-free, quick quilting methods, you could certainly break out your straw needles and hand appliqué this elegant beauty. I encourage you to use the method that brings you the most satisfaction and joy.

FABRIC SUGGESTIONS

Choose a dark floral print for the outside border and a complementary geometric print for the inner border. While the prints should be close in value, they need to show a definite shift in value towards the very light quilt center. The cornerstone should be the darkest print to accentuate the corners and blend out to the darkest value in the binding.

GATHERING YOUR FABRICS

You will need six fabrics for this quilt plus backing. The yardages are based on 40" usable width of fabric.

A	Dark	¼ yard	white-on-black, large-scale floral print for outer border
B	Medium	¼ yard	white-on-black, medium-scale grid print for inner border
C	Very dark	⅛ yard	white-on-black, large-scale print for cornerstones
D	Light	⅓ yard	white solid for quilt center
E	Solid black	½ yard	for posy stem, base, leaves, and binding
F	Vibrant orange/red batik	⅛ yard for petals	
Backing		¾ yard	
Batting		22" x 36½"	
Paper-backed fusible web		¼ yard	

CUTTING INSTRUCTIONS

Strips are cut across the width of the fabric unless stated otherwise.

Fabric A   2 strips 3" wide cut into
            2 strips 3" x 27½"
            2 strips 3" x 13"

Fabric B   2 strips 3" wide cut into
            2 strips 3" x 22½"
            2 strips 3" x 13"

Fabric C   1 strip 3" wide cut into
            4 squares 3" x 3"

Fabric D   1 strip 8" wide cut into
            1 rectangle 8" x 22½"

Fabric E   1 strip 16½" wide cut into
            1 bias strip 1¼" wide
            1 square 16" x 16"

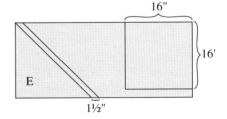

SEWING INSTRUCTIONS

Sew the fabric B 3" x 22½" strips to the top and bottom of the fabric D rectangle. Press the seams toward the border.

Add the fabric B 3" x 13" strips to the sides. Press the seams toward the border.

Sew the fabric A 3" x 27½" strips to the top and bottom. Press the seams toward the border.

Sew a fabric C square to both ends of the fabric A 3" x 13" strips. Press the seams toward the border and then add to the sides.

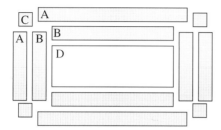

Trace the already reversed blossom petals, flower base, and leaves on paper-backed fusible web. Cut out ⅛" outside the traced line.

Place the fusible web petals on the wrong side of fabric F and the flower base and leaves on fabric E. Fuse the pieces to the fabrics following the manufacturer's instructions. Cut out all the pieces on the drawn lines.

Arrange the petals as shown and fuse in place.

Fold the fabric E bias strip in half lengthwise, wrong sides together, and press carefully without stretching.

Arrange the bias stem in gentle curves as shown.

Mark the stem curve on the quilt. Line up the raw edges of the bias stem with the marked line and pin the stem in place, easing in fullness.

Stitch the stem to the quilt ¼" in from the raw edges.

Fold the stem back over the seam and gently press, easing in fullness.

Machine stitch the stem down with invisible thread. Add the leaves and flower base and fuse in place.

Layer the quilt top with the backing and batting, then quilt the layers by hand or machine.

Make continuous binding from the 16" square and bind the edges of the quilt.

FINISHING TOUCHES

I did not do any hand or machine stitching to secure the petals. I prefer the ease and speed of utilizing the quilting to add texture and firmly hold them in place.

While I enjoy the occasional blurry or fuzzy edge of raw-edge machine appliqué, you may prefer the more polished look of machine appliquéing prior to quilting.

Allover free-motion quilting echoes the points and curves of the blossom.

I used white thread in the quilt center and switched to black for the borders. I let little tips of black sneak out into the white quilt center to soften the leap from the dark border to the very light background.

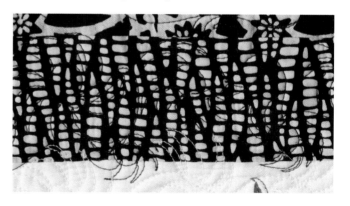

BALINESE BEAUTY

Template

Kay M. Capps Cross

BALINESE BEAUTY

18" x 34", pieced and quilted by the author. *Fabric courtesy of Bali Fabric, Inc.*

This version of the quilt has the advantage of color flowing from the center out through the borders. Melding hues allows the quilt to shift elegantly with no hard edges. Less contrast between the center of the quilt and the borders adds fluidity.

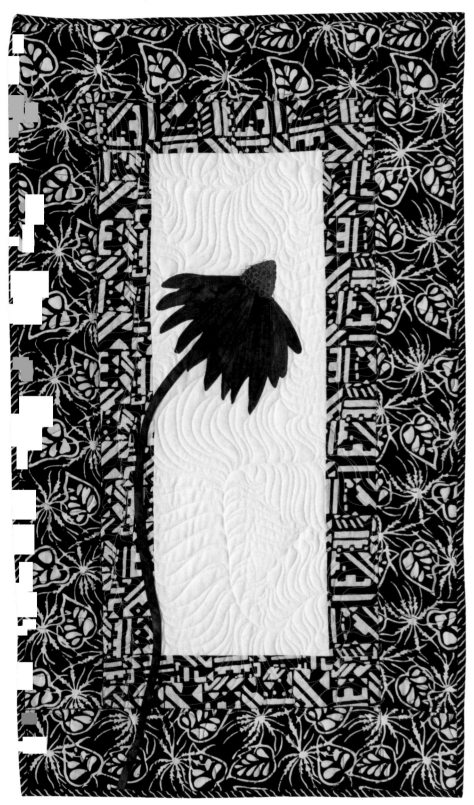

CONEY
22" x 38"

TRIUNE

Pieced and quilted by the author.
Fabric courtesy of Bali Fabric, Inc.

Individually, the pieces in TRIUNE
are lovely, but together they create a
collection of simple beauty to bring
the garden indoors. Embellished or
not, they sparkle with the promise
of spring's renewal. The restorative
power of beautiful blossoms is
remarkable. Install a garden gallery to
provide outdoor beauty every day.

The simple frame piecing makes
creating the collection a snap. With
fusible appliqué speeding up the
process, there will still be time to till
the soil come spring.

LIL' DARLIN'
16" x 16"

PANSY
14½" x 21½"

FABRIC SUGGESTIONS

Choose a clear and distinct large floral print for the outside border of CONEY. Pair it with a strong geometric print for the inner border. Select an almost stripe-like print for piecing the LIL' DARLIN' checkerboard border and a classy medium print for the PANSY border. Light white for the background provides the most drama while the striped flannel zinger border adds flair. Choose batiks with a wide color range for the posies. CONEY's tip is from an orange section of the same medium fabric used for the other flowers. More variation in value will provide movement and offer you more choices.

GATHERING YOUR FABRICS

You will need eight fabrics for this three-in-one quilt plus backing and binding. The yardages are based on 40" usable width of fabric.

A	Medium dark	¾ yard	white-on-black, large-scale leaf print for the CONEY outer border
B	Medium dark	¼ yard	white-on-black, medium-scale spiky leaf print for the LIL' DARLIN' checkerboard
C	Medium dark	¼ yard	white-on-black, medium-scale water lily print for the LIL' DARLIN' checkerboard
D	Medium dark	¼ yard	white-on-black, large-scale geometric print for the CONEY inner border
E	Light	⅝ yard	solid white for quilt centers
F	Dark	½ yard	purple batik for the stems and the posies
G	Medium	⅛ yard	purple/fuchsia/orange striped flannel batik for PANSY zinger inner border
H	Medium	⅛ yard	vibrant fuchsia/orange batik for the posies
Backing		1½ yards	
Binding		¾ yard	dark, white-on-black stripe
Batting		26" x 46" (CONEY) • 20" x 20" (LIL' DARLIN') • 18½" x 25½" (PANSY)	
Paper-backed fusible web		¼ yard	

CUTTING INSTRUCTIONS

Strips are cut across the width of the fabric unless stated otherwise.

Fabric A	4 strips 4½" wide cut into
	2 strips 4½" x 30"
	2 strips 4½" x 22"
	2 strips 2½" wide
Fabric B	2 strips 2½" wide
Fabric C	2 strips 3½" wide cut into
	2 strips 3½" x 8½"
	2 strips 3½" x 21½"
Fabric D	2 strips 3" wide cut into
	2 strips 3" x 25"
	2 strips 3" x 14"
Fabric E	1 strip 9" wide cut into 1 rectangle 9" x 25" (CONEY)
	1 strip 8½" wide cut into
	1 square 8½" x 8½" (LIL' DARLIN')
	1 rectangle 8½" x 15 ½" (PANSY)
Fabric F	2 bias strips 1¼" wide
Fabric G	2 strips 1½" wide cut into
	2 strips 1½" x 8½"
	2 strips 1½" x 15½"
Binding	1 square 24" x 24" for 2¼" continuous binding

SEWING INSTRUCTIONS

Making the Background

You will be building three quilt canvases for the posies. Each one has a little different twist.

CONEY *has two simple borders.*

Sew the 2 fabric D 3" x 25" strips to the sides of the fabric E 9" x 25" rectangle. Press the seams toward the strips.

Sew the 2 fabric D 3" x 14" strips to the top and bottom. Press.

In the same way, add the 2 fabric A 4½" x 30" strips to the sides and the 2 fabric A 4½" x 22" strips to the top and bottom. Press the seams toward the strips.

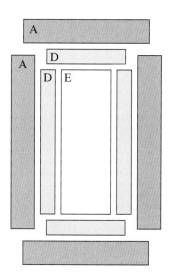

Lil' Darlin' *has a checkerboard border.*

Make 2 strip-sets, each with a 2½" strip of fabric A and fabric B. Press the seam allowances toward fabric B.

Cut 24 segments 2½" wide from the strip-sets.

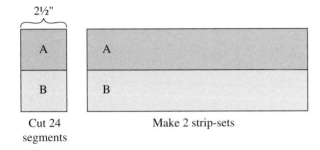

Cut 24 segments

Make 2 strip-sets

Join 2 segments to make a four-patch unit. Make 12.

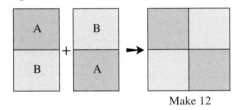

Make 12

Arrange the four-patch units around the fabric E 8½" square, keeping fabric A in the same upper left hand spot all the way around.

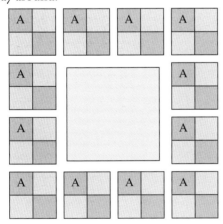

Sew 2 four-patch units together and add to the sides of the square.

Sew 4 four-patch units together and add to the top and bottom. Press the seams in toward the center.

Pansy *has a zinger inner border within the outer border.*

Fold the 4 fabric G 1½" strips in half lengthwise, wrong sides together, and press.

Align the raw edges of the 8½" folded strips with the sides of the fabric E 8½" x 15½" rectangle and sew using a ⅛" seam allowance.

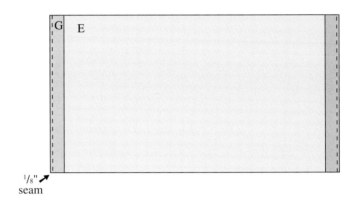

⅛"
seam

In the same manner, align the raw edges of the 15½" folded strips with the top and bottom of the rectangle and sew using a ⅛" seam allowance. Press the strips flat toward the center of the quilt.

Sew the fabric C 3½" x 8½"" strips to the sides, sandwiching the zinger border. Press the strips outward, leaving the zinger border flat against the background.

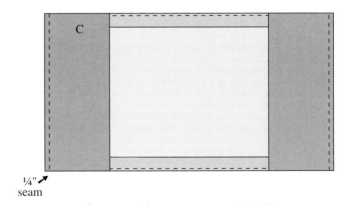

¼"
seam

In the same manner, add the fabric C 3½" x 21½" strips to the top and bottom.

Adding the Blossoms

Choose the lightest section of fabric H for the center of Coney and the egg shape of Lil' Darlin'. Use the darker parts of the same fabric for the Pansy petals. Cut all other pieces from fabric F.

Trace the already reversed posy parts and leaves on paper-backed fusible web. Cut out ⅛" beyond the traced line (see pages 58–59).

Place the fusible-web posy parts and leaves on the wrong side of the appropriate fabrics and fuse following the manufacturer's instructions.

Cut out the posy parts and leaves exactly on the traced lines.

Join the 2 fabric F 1¼" bias strips end-to-end. Press the seams open. Fold the strip in half lengthwise, wrong sides together, and press carefully without stretching.

Arrange the bias stems in gentle curves on the Coney quilt as shown in the quilt photo, page 52. Mark the stem curve on the block and pin the stem in place, easing in fullness and trimming the excess.

Align the raw edges of the bias stem with the marked line and stitch with a ¼" seam allowance.

Fold the stem back over the seam and gently press, easing in fullness.

Machine stitch the edge of the stem down with invisible thread.

In the same way, add a stem to Lil' Darlin'.

Referring to the quilt photo, arrange the posy parts and leaves for each quilt and fuse in place following the manufacturer's instructions, making sure to cover the ends of the stems.

FINISHING TOUCHES

Layer the three quilt tops with backing and batting, then quilt the layers by hand or machine.

Make continuous binding from the 24" square and bind the edges of the quilts.

I did not do any hand or machine stitching to secure the posies before machine quilting right over the petals to secure them.

Pansy got some heavy machine quilting in the flower center to add dimension and light. Diagonal lines cross the background and parallel straight lines fill the border. The flannel zinger border is kept loose and is not quilted down.

Coney is surrounded by a pointy fern wreath with large licorice whips in the large-scale border. The variation in quilting density allows the border to be fuller and the center of the quilt to recede. The center of the flower is accented by small circular quilting to bring out the orange cone.

Lil' Darlin' echoes the circular quilting in its egg-shaped center and parallel lines defining the petals. An allover swirly pattern blends the piecing in the checkerboard with the pure white background.

I avoided embellishments to capitalize on the beauty of the fabrics and retain the crisp clean essence of the three quilts.

LIL' DARLIN'
16" x 16", pieced and quilted by the author.
Fabric courtesy of Bali Fabric, Inc.

Enlarge 200%

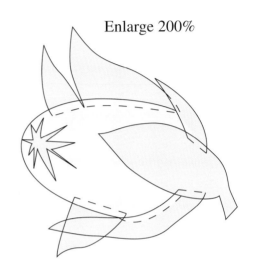

PANSY
14½" x 21½", pieced and quilted by the author.
Fabric courtesy of Bali Fabric, Inc.

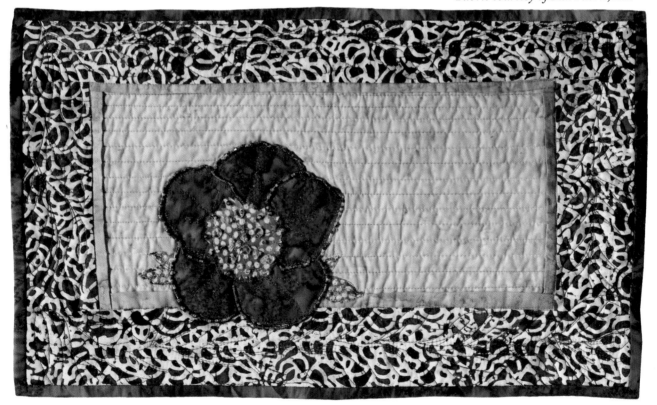

Kay M. Capps Cross

CONEY

22" x 38", pieced and quilted by the author.

Fabric courtesy of Bali Fabric, Inc.

Enlarge 200%

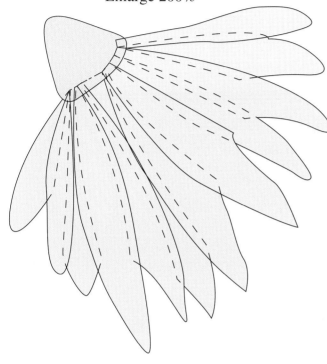

Enlarge 200%

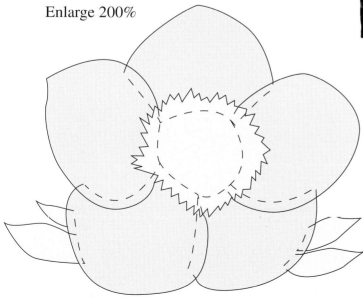

GARDEN GODDESSES

56" x 72", pieced and quilted by the author.

Kay M. Capps Cross

I'm drawn to seemingly random patches of color in gardens. Order amid chaos creates a spare yet polished setting for the vivid blooms in this quilt. The simple piecing frames and highlights the solitary sparks of color. In an effort to maintain this clean and bright garden, all leaves have been confined to one block. No messy raking, no tricky piecing or time-consuming handwork is needed to create this garden. Fusible appliqué provides the speedy growing season!

FABRIC SUGGESTIONS

I used black-and-white batiks to contrast with the solid white for this quilt. The flat white provides a pure blank canvas for the vivid blossoms. To match and balance the vigorous blooms, a mixture of black-and-white prints of varying scales provides interest and movement. Choose fabrics that are similar in value but range greatly in scale. Small-scale stripes or grid prints work well to spice up the mix, and floral prints in different scales add movement. Geometric prints always add a punch. Well thought out fabric choices will produce a diverse and interesting garden.

GATHERING YOUR FABRICS

You will need a minimum of 5 fabrics for this quilt plus backing, but I recommend a mix of large- and medium-scale white-on-black prints. The yardages are based on 40" usable width of fabric.

A	Light	1¾ yards	white solid for block centers
B	Medium dark	2¼ yards total	white-on-black, large-scale prints for borders and spacers
C	Medium dark	1⅛ yards total	white-on-black, medium-scale prints for borders
D	Dark solid black	¾ yard	flowers, stems, and binding
E	Dark red, red, and vibrant orange/red batiks	½ yard total for flowers	
Backing	4¾ yards		
Batting	64" x 80"		
Paper-backed fusible web 12" wide	2⅓ yards		

CUTTING INSTRUCTIONS

Strips are cut across width of fabric unless otherwise stated.

Fabric A for the block backgrounds
    2 strips 8½" wide cut into
        1 square 8½" x 8½" (block 12)
        1 rectangle 8½" x 22½" (block 2)
    1 strip 7½" wide cut into
        1 rectangle 7½" x 16" (block 13)
    5 strips 8" wide cut into
        1 rectangle 8" x 23" (block 11)
        2 rectangles 8" x 22½" (blocks 8 and 10)
        1 rectangle 8" x 20" (block 1)
        1 rectangle 8" x 15½" (block 7)
        1 rectangle 8" x 10½" (block 6)
        3 squares 8" x 8" (blocks 3, 4, and 5)
        1 rectangle 8" x 3" (block 9)

Fabric B for the borders and spacers
    1 strip 6½" wide (block 10 spacer)
    1 strip 5" wide (block 11 spacer)
    1 strip 4½" wide (block 11 spacer)

Fabric B (continued)
    4 strips 3½" wide (borders for blocks 1 and 7)
    10 strips 3" wide (borders)
    3 strips 2½" wide (2 for block 12 borders,
        1 for block 1 spacer)
    3 strips 1¾" wide (checkerboard borders)
    2 strips 1½" wide (block 8, 9, 10, and 12 spacers)
    1 strip 1" wide (block 3 spacers)

Set aside the spacer strips until you are ready to join the finished blocks.

Fabric C for the borders and cornerstones
    9 strips 3" wide (borders)
    2 strips 2½" wide (block 12 border)
    3 strips 1¾" wide (checkerboard borders)

Fabric D
    1 strip 25" wide cut into
        1 square 25" x 25" for 2¼" continuous bias binding
        10 bias strips 1¼" wide for stems

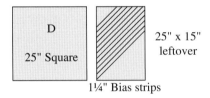

SEWING INSTRUCTIONS

Making the Blocks

Blocks #1, 2, 4, 6, 7, 8, 9, and 11, are framed by a single border.

Block 13 has a second border.

Block # & Name	Block Center	Orientation	Border Fabric	Strip Width
1. Trumpet	20" x 8"	H	fabric B	3½"
2. Bearded	8½" x 22½"	V	fabric C	3"
4. Tulip	8" x 8"	S	fabric C	3"
6. Alpine	8" x 10½"	V	fabric B	3"
7. Starflower	8" x 15½"	V	fabric B	3½"
8. Paradise	8" x 22½"	V	fabric B	3"
9. Leaves	8" x 3"	H	fabric B	3"
11. Poppy	8" x 23"	V	fabric C	3"
13. Open Tulip	7½" x 16"	V	fabric B	3"
			fabric C	3"

Cut segments the width of the fabric A center blocks from the strips indicated. Sew them to the top and bottom. Press the seam allowances toward the strips. Pay attention to the orientation of each block.

Measure the length of the blocks including the borders, cut strips to that measurement, and sew them to the sides of each block. Press.

Repeat these steps for the second block 13 border.

Label the bordered blocks.

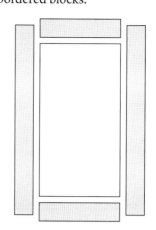

Block #10 has two borders with cornerstones on the second border.

Block # & Name	Center	Orientation	Border Fabric	Strip Width
10. Calla Lily	22½" x 8"	H ▭	fabric C	3"
			fabric B	3" with fabric C cornerstones

Add fabric C 3" strips to all sides of the fabric A rectangle.

Cut 4 fabric C 3" x 3" cornerstone squares.

Measure the height (short end) of the block.

Cut two fabric B 3" strips to that measurement and add the cornerstones to both ends of both strips.

Add fabric B 3" strips to the top and bottom (long sides) of the block. Then add the strips with cornerstone units to the sides. Label the block.

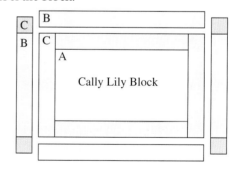

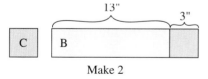

Make 2

Blocks # 3, 5, and 12 have a 4-patch checkerboard border.

Block # & Name	Center	Orientation	Border Fabric	Strip Width
3. Sunflower	8" x 8"	S □	4-patch checkerboard fabrics B & C	1¾"
5. Coneflower	8" x 8"	S □	4-patch checkerboard fabrics B & C	1¾"
12. Bellflower	8½" x 8½"	S □	4-patch checkerboard fabrics B & C	2½"

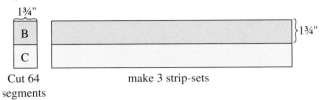
Make 3 strip-sets with fabrics B and C 1¾" strips. Cut 64 segments 1¾" wide.

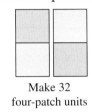

1¾"

B
C

1¾"

Cut 64 segments

make 3 strip-sets

Join 2 segments to make a 4-patch unit. Make 32.

Make 32 four-patch units

Keeping fabric B in the upper-left corner of each 4-patch unit, arrange 16 units around a fabric A 8" square. Join 3 units for the sides and 5 units for the top and bottom. Add to the square. Repeat for the second fabric A 8" square.

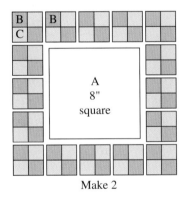

B
C

B

A
8"
square

Make 2

Label the Sunflower and Coneflower blocks.

Make 2 strip-sets with fabrics B and C 2½" strips. Cut 24 segments 2½" wide.

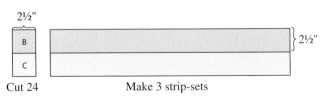

2½"

B

C

2½"

Cut 24

Make 3 strip-sets

Join 2 segments to make a 4-patch unit. Make 12.

Make 12 four-patch units

Keeping fabric B in the upper-left corner of each 4-patch unit, arrange 12 units around a fabric A 8½" square. Join 2 units for each side and 4 units for the top and bottom. Add to the square.

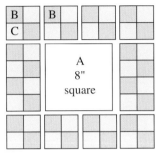

B
C

B

A
8"
square

Label the Bellflower block.

Adding the Stems, Flowers, and Leaves

Join the fabric D 1¼" bias strips end-to-end and press the seams open.

Fold the strip in half lengthwise, wrong sides together, and press carefully without stretching.

Referring to the photograph of the quilt on page 60, arrange the stems in gentle curves for each block as shown, trimming off the excess. Stitch the stems to the blocks ¼" in from the raw edges. Fold each stem back over the seam and gently press, easing in fullness. Machine stitch the stems down with invisible thread.

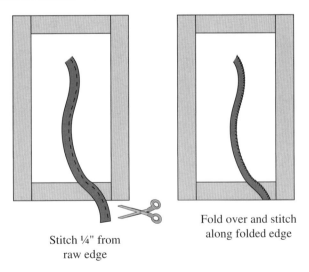

Stitch ¼" from raw edge

Fold over and stitch along folded edge

Trace the already reversed flowers and leaves templates (pages 66–77) on paper-backed fusible web. Cut out ⅛" outside the traced line.

Place the "color" flowers on the wrong side of the assorted E fabrics and the "black" flower parts and leaves on the wrong side of fabric D. Fuse, following the manufacturer's instructions. Cut out exactly on the traced line.

Referring to the figure on page 64, arrange the flower parts and leaves, making sure the ends of the stems are hidden beneath the flowers and fuse in place.

Join the blocks into units, as shown below, adding spacer strips where indicated, then sew the units together.

Layer the quilt top with the backing and batting, then quilt the layers by hand or machine.

Make continuous binding from the 25" square and bind the edges of the quilt.

FINISHING TOUCHES

I did not do any hand or machine stitching to secure the posies. I prefer the ease and speed of utilizing the quilting to add texture and hold the petals and leaves in place.

I had great fun altering the quilting according to what each flower told me it wanted. Poppy and Paradise have strong vertical lines to add height. Open Tulip and Tulip have rounded leaves that mimic the fabric in Tulip's frame. Pointy leaves and swirls fill Starflower, Calla Lily, Trumpet and Bellflower. Starflower and Bearded are highlighted with echo quilting and Sunflower and Coneflower are surrounded by pointy zigzags. Some of the borders get individual treatment and some are absorbed into the whole block.

Experiment and infuse your quilt with texture and movement that enhance the piecing but don't overwhelm it.

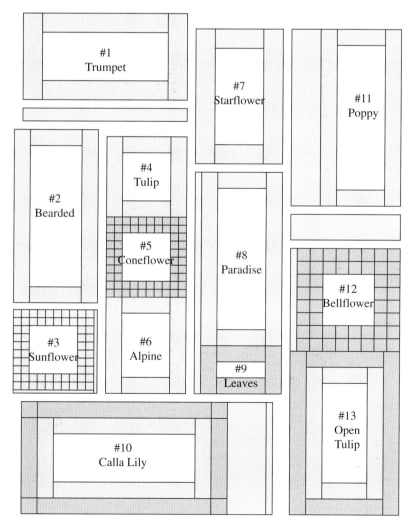

TRUMPET – BLOCK 1

Kay M. Capps Cross

BEARDED – BLOCK 2

TULIP – BLOCK 4

Kay M. Capps Cross

SUNFLOWER – BLOCK 3

CONEFLOWER – BLOCK 5

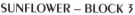

ALPINE – BLOCK 6

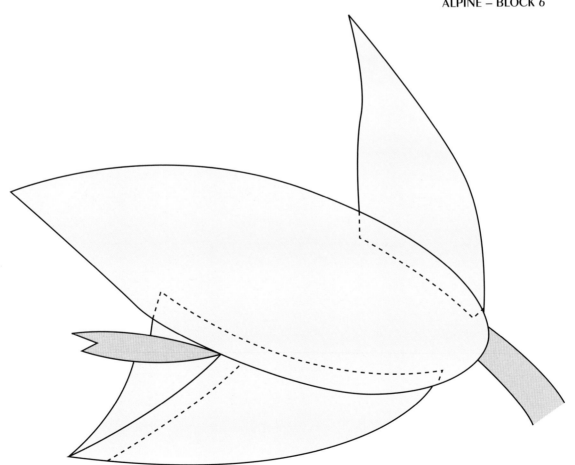

STARFLOWER – BLOCK 7

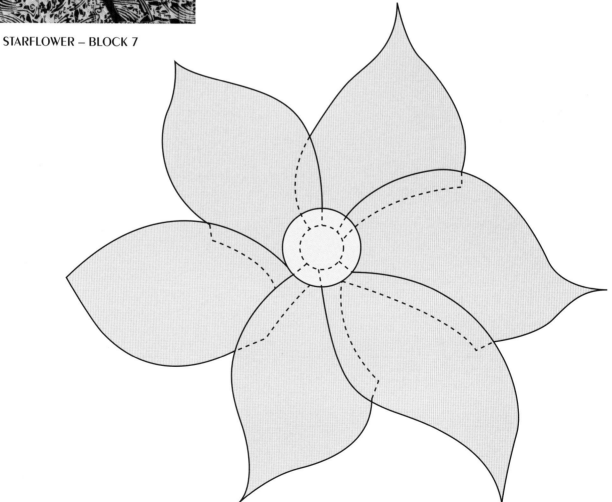

PARADISE – BLOCK 8

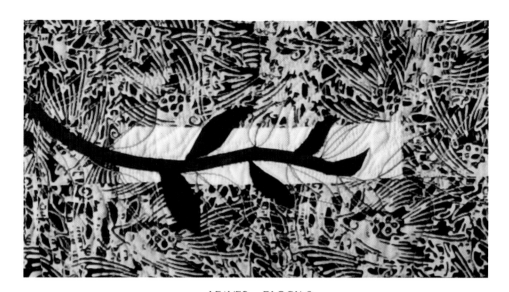

LEAVES – BLOCK 9

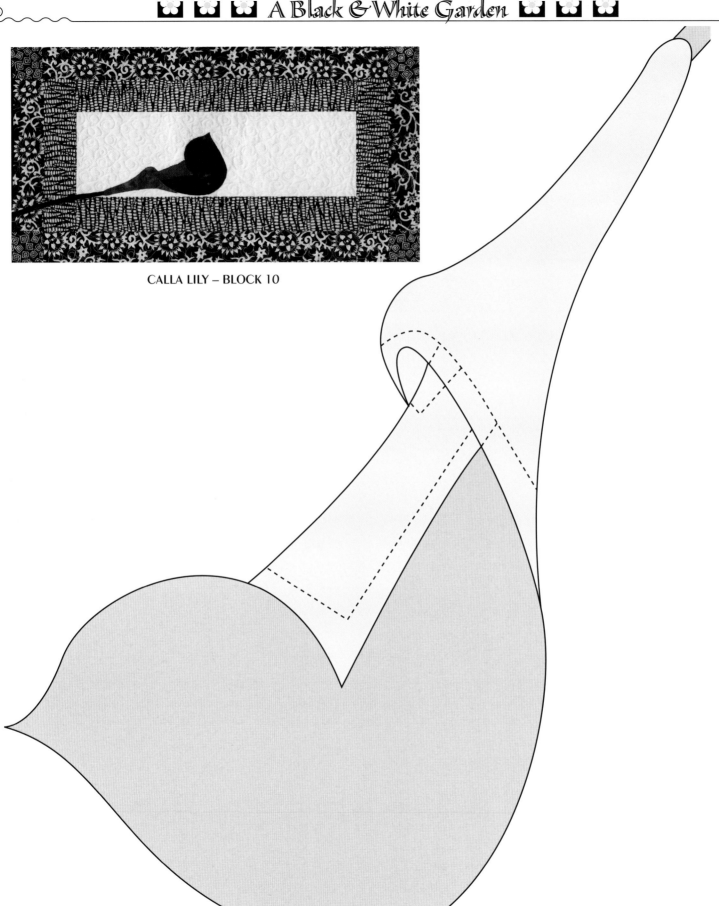

CALLA LILY – BLOCK 10

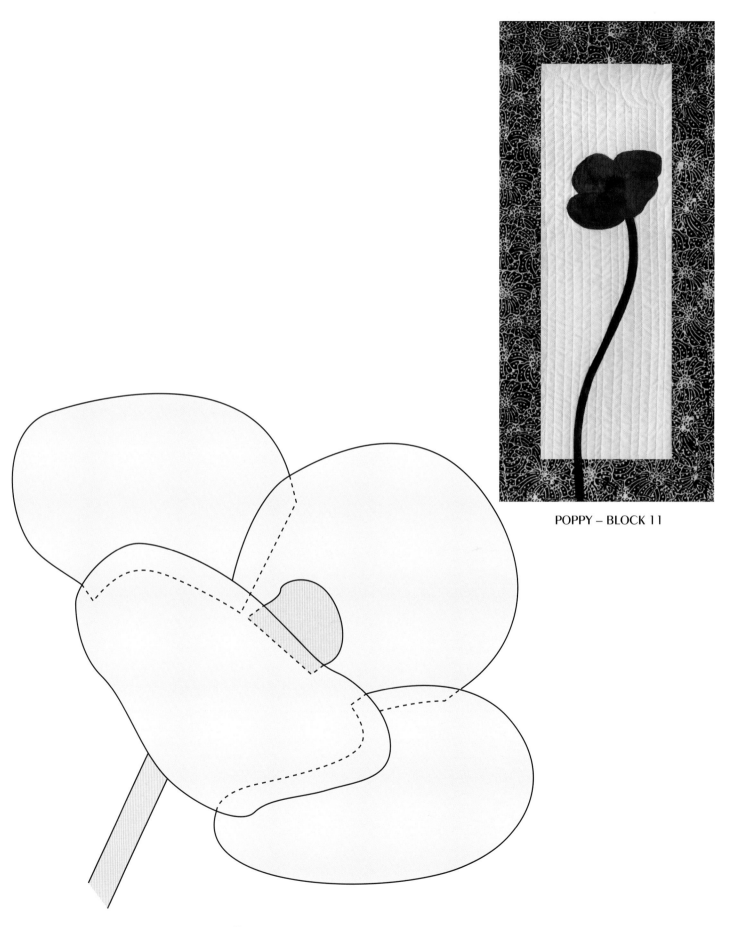

POPPY – BLOCK 11

BELLFLOWER – BLOCK 12

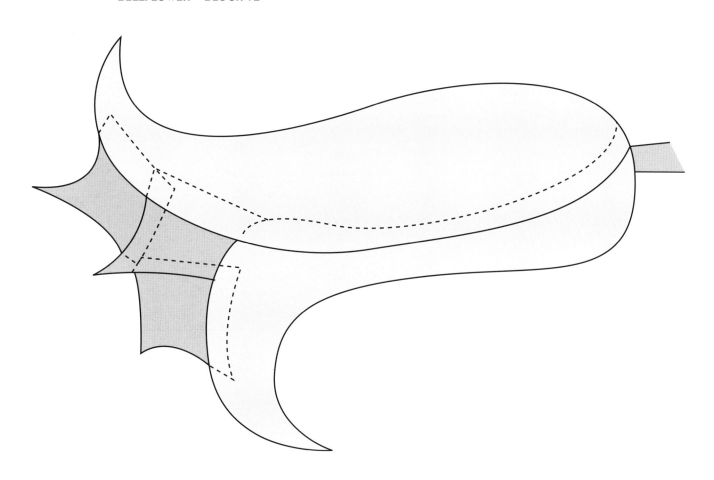

OPEN TULIP – BLOCK 13

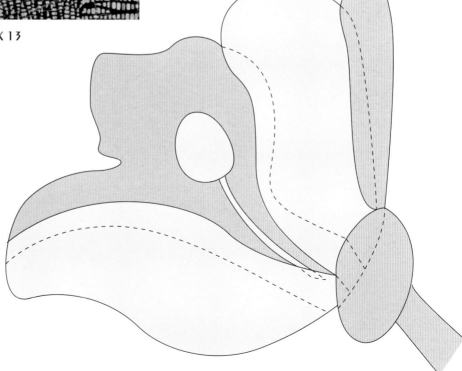

RESOURCES

Fabrics

Bali Fabrics, Inc.
21787 8th St. East #1
Sonoma, CA 95476
Phone: 800-783-4612
Fax: 866-233-9117
Web site: www.balifab.com

Island Batik, Inc.
2719 Loker Avenue West, Suite B
Carlsbad, CA 92008
Phone: 888-522-2845
Fax: 760-602-0609
Web site: www.islandbatik.com

Telegraph Road Studio
a division of David Textiles, Inc.
1920 S. Tubeway Ave.
City of Commerce, Ca 90040
Phone: 800-548-1818
Fax: 323-725-6710
Web site: www.davidtextilesinc.com

Silks, Indian Trims and Squares

Shobha Imports
5795 Forbees Dr.
Newark, CA 94560
Phone: 570-794-1284
kuldipshodan@yahoo.com

ABOUT THE AUTHOR

photo by Melissa Vander Plas, Harmony, MN

It is hard to believe I am writing "About the Author" for my second book. How did I get to this wonderful place? I have been so fortunate in this journey. I happened into the quilting world by chance and what a happy accident it has been. Making clothes for my children led me to a quilt shop, which eventually grabbed me by the nose and led me to the life of a quilter/teacher/author. Thank you for letting me choose a sewing machine instead of a typewriter for graduation, Mom. It has served me well.

My quilting life is spent creating, writing, and teaching. I have been fortunate to have quilts appear in *Fabric Trends, McCall's Quilting, McCall's Quick Quilts, Quilter's World, American Quilter,* and *Professional Quilter*. My first book, *Black & White Quilts by Design,* was published by AQS. My patterns are distributed internationally and my travels take me to retreats, guilds, shops, and shows around the country. I enjoy meeting, teaching, and learning from folks from all over. Sharing my love of black and white along with stress-free quilting is such a gift for me. Along with a fulfilling life in quilting, I actually have a personal life, too!

In my "real" life, my husband and I spend many hours a week improving our bleacher bottoms. We have four children active in a plethora of academic, musical, theatrical, and sporting activities and I wouldn't trade a second of it. It seems impossible some days to fit it all in, but I am blessed with a wonderful family who does not begrudge me the time to follow and embrace my passion. They know that they are my priority, so they let me out like a yo-yo to play and then yank me back to sit on the bleachers some more! Life couldn't be better.

I truly admire quilters who create heirloom quilts for future generations to treasure. Someday I may do that, but for now I'll utilize methods that leave me time for my personal heirloom creations: Garrett, Kaley, Addison, and Elliott.

Other AQS Books

This is only a small selection of the books available from the American Quilter's Society. AQS books are known worldwide for timely topics, clear writing, beautiful color photos, and accurate illustrations and patterns. The following books are available from your local bookseller, quilt shop, or public library.

#6902 US$22.95	#7601 US$26.95	#7486 US$22.95
#7078 US$24.95	#7073 US$24.95	#7602 US$26.95
#7604 US$24.95	#7600 US$26.95	#7615 US$24.95

Look for these books nationally.
Call or **Visit** our Web site at

1-800-626-5420
www.AmericanQuilter.com